YAS

Maya Angelou

Maya Angelou

Author and Documentary Filmmaker

LUCIA RAATMA

Ferguson Publishing Company
Chicago, Illinois

Photographs ©: AP/Wideworld: 17, 38–39, 44, 57, 59, 65, 74, 80, 82, 86, 88, 91, 92, 98; Archive: 10, 24–25, 32, 36, 40–41, 58, 61, 63, 68, 77; Corbis: 14, 18–19, 50, 51, 56, 81, 95

An Editorial Directions Book

Library of Congress Cataloging-in-Publication Data
Raatma, Lucia.
Maya Angelou: writer and documentary filmmaker / by Lucia Raatma.
p. cm. — (Ferguson's career biographies)
Includes bibliographical references and index.
    ISBN 0-89434-336-X
    1. Angelou, Maya—Juvenile literature. 2. Authors, American—20th century—Biography—Juvenile literature. 3. Motion picture producers and directors—Biography—Juvenile literature. 4. Entertainers—United States—Biography—Juvenile literature. 5. Afro-American women authors—Biography—Juvenile literature. [1. Angelou, Maya. 2. Authors, American. 3. Afro-Americans—Biography. 4. Women—Biography] I. Title. II. Series.
PS3551.N464 Z83 2000
818'5409—dc21
[B]   00-037582

Copyright © 2000 by Ferguson Publishing Company
Published and distributed by
Ferguson Publishing Company
200 West Jackson Boulevard, Suite 700
Chicago, Illinois 60606
www.fergpubco.com

Printed in the United States of America
X-8

CONTENTS

Maya Angelou

THE POWER OF WORDS

MAYA ANGELOU'S EARLY life was difficult. But rather than allowing her problems to drag her down, Angelou has risen above them.

Many times, Angelou could have given up. She could have decided that life was too hard or that people were too hateful. As an African-American woman, many obstacles stood in her way. But she always found time to read, to learn about the world around her. And even as a child, she wrote about her own life.

The power of Maya Angelou's words have had an impact throughout the world.

She wrote about the days that were sad. And she wrote about the people she loved. At the time, her essays and poems may have been only scribbles in a notebook. But they marked the beginnings of one of the most important writers in the United States.

Throughout her life, Angelou was always curious and intelligent. She tried to understand the people around her. But often they were hard to understand. And sometimes the actions of others frustrated her. Nevertheless, she didn't give up on other people or on herself. Now, when she gives advice to the young people she meets, she tells them, "You might encounter many defeats, but you must never be defeated."

Today, Maya Angelou is known as a gifted poet, a renowned screenwriter and director, a performer, and a social activist. She has used the power of her mind and the power of her words to make her life extraordinary.

LOOKING FOR HOME

MAYA ANGELOU WAS born on April 4, 1928, in St. Louis, Missouri. The name she was given was Marguerite Annie Johnson. A few years later, when she was living with her parents and her brother, Bailey, in California, everything changed.

Her parents decided their marriage was not working out. And neither her mother nor her father felt able to care for their children at that time. So at the age of three, young Marguerite was placed on a train with her brother, who was then four. Both of

St. Louis in the late 1920s. Maya was born there but soon moved to California and then to Arkansas.

them wore name tags that said they were going to Stamps, Arkansas, to meet Annie Henderson, their grandmother.

The trip must have been frightening for both Marguerite and Bailey. They didn't know anyone on the train. And they didn't know why they were being sent away from their parents. A few other African-American passengers were friendly to them though. They shared their food with the lonely children and tried to look after them. Finally, Marguerite and Bailey reached Arkansas, and a new part of their lives began.

Life in Stamps

Stamps, Arkansas, was a small town close to the Louisiana border. The town was divided into two distinct sections—a white section and a black section. When Marguerite and Bailey arrived there—and for many years afterward—the two sections remained entirely separate. At that time, most of the South was separated in this way. White people and black people ate in different parts of restaurants and rode in different parts of buses. They even had to drank from separate water fountains.

African-Americans were expected to respect white people and never to argue with them. Members of the Ku Klux Klan had killed many black men in Stamps. The Ku Klux Klan was racist. Members believed that whites were superior to blacks. No one was safe from the racists around them.

Growing up, Marguerite became used to the differences between her world and the world of white people. But she never felt the differences were fair. She knew that blacks deserved the same rights as whites.

Sometimes white people seemed so foreign to her that Marguerite didn't quite believe they were real. Years later, she wrote, "People were those who lived on my side of town. I didn't like them all, or, in fact, any of them very much, but they were people. These others, the strange pale creatures that lived in

A Ku Klux Klan rally in 1936. This group believes that white people are superior to all other races.

their alien unlife, weren't considered folks. They were white folks."

Grandmother Henderson

Annie Henderson was Marguerite and Bailey's grandmother. Her sons were Bailey Johnson Sr., their father, and William Johnson, known to them as Uncle Willie. Soon after Marguerite and Bailey moved in with her, they stopped calling her "Grandmother." To them, she became simply "Momma."

Momma was tall and strong. She had been married three times—once to Mr. Johnson, her sons' father, then to Mr. Henderson, and then to Mr. Murphy. Young Marguerite knew very little about these men, and Momma seldom spoke of them.

*Annie Henderson cared for her grandchildren in a rural section
of Arkansas where she owned a general store.*

Momma had learned to support herself and to take care of her family. She owned the Wm. Johnson General Merchandise Store in Stamps. People from the black section of town shopped and talked at the Store, as it was called. It was a gathering place and the center of activity.

Maya and Bailey

Marguerite and Bailey were very close and quite devoted to each other. In Stamps, they settled into a routine and got used to living with Momma. Along the way, Bailey started calling his sister "my sister" and sometimes just "my." Before long, this nickname changed to "Maya." So Marguerite became Maya to many of her family members.

Maya was a smart girl but sometimes she was shy. She told all her secrets only to Bailey. He was also bright and very attractive. People always liked Bailey and listened to what he said.

Maya worried about how she looked. She was taller than most of the kids, her long legs were skinny, and her hair stuck out in places. But when people teased her about her appearance, Bailey always stuck up for her. And he told her she was the most beautiful person he had ever seen.

As Maya later wrote, "Bailey was the greatest person in my world. And the fact that he was my brother, my only brother, and I had no sisters to share him with, was such good fortune that it made me want to live a Christian life just to show God that I was grateful."

Home Life

Momma was a very strict woman, and she expected a lot from her grandchildren. Maya and Bailey wanted to please Momma so they studied hard for school, and they worked in the Store too. Momma was also very religious. She taught Maya and Bailey Bible stories, and she took them to church every Sunday.

Momma also taught them to respect adults and to remember their manners. She never hesitated to punish the children if they were rude to adults or if they misbehaved.

She also expected them to be neat and clean. Even in the coldest weather, Maya and Bailey had to use the chilly water from the well outside to wash up each night. But no matter how hard the rules seemed to be, Maya and Bailey always knew that Momma loved them.

Faraway Parents

For years, Maya and Bailey wondered why they had been sent away from their parents. They did not understand divorce, and they wondered whether their parents loved them. For a time, they even convinced themselves that their parents were dead, because they never heard from them.

But one Christmas, all that changed. Maya and Bailey got Christmas presents from their mother and father—each sent from a different address. Instead of being happy about these gifts, Maya and Bailey were very upset. Maya went out into the yard and cried. Very soon, Bailey joined her. They wondered how their parents could send presents but not come to visit them. And they wondered why they lived so far away.

A Visit from Their Father

Then one day in 1935, they did get a visit. Bailey Johnson Sr. drove up in a big fancy car. He was very tall and wore expensive clothes. Maya and Bailey couldn't believe how handsome their father was.

Bailey Sr. did not speak like the people in Stamps did. His way of speaking was very proper and he did not have a southern accent. He talked about California and how warm it was there.

Then, after visiting for a few weeks, he said he was taking Maya and Bailey with him. Bailey was excited, he wanted to move to California. But Maya was scared. She didn't remember any life other than the one she had with Momma in Stamps and she was afraid to leave her grandmother. At one point as she prepared to leave Stamps, Maya asked Momma if she loved her. Momma didn't answer the question directly but said, "God is love. Just worry about whether you are being a good girl, then He will love you." In spite of that indirect response, Maya left Stamps knowing that Momma's love would follow her.

Maya and Bailey packed their things and said good-bye to Momma. Once in their father's car, however, they discovered they were not going to California after all. He was taking them to St. Louis to live with their mother.

In St. Louis

St. Louis was nothing like the small town of Stamps. St. Louis was a loud and bustling city, while Stamps had been quiet. Maya and Bailey couldn't believe how different city life was.

Once they arrived in St. Louis, Maya and Bailey were taken to their Grandmother Baxter's house. Grandmother Baxter was an important woman. She had influence over many people in St. Louis, including the city's police force. Maya and Bailey worried about whether or not their grandmother would like them. But they worried even more about meeting their mother, Vivian Baxter. They didn't remember much about her. And they also wondered what this woman, who had sent them away five years before, would be like.

After living in Stamps, Maya and her brother were shocked by how different life was in the big city of St. Louis.

When Vivian Baxter walked into the room at her mother's house, Maya and Bailey couldn't believe what they saw. To them, she was beautiful. She had light-brown skin and perfect red lips. Bailey said she was prettier than the white movie stars.

For six months, Maya and Bailey lived with Grandmother Baxter and her four sons. These four uncles were big and tough. They worked for the city and were well known around their neighborhood. Many people were afraid of them, but they were always kind to Maya and Bailey.

Another Change

Then, after those six months, Maya and Bailey moved in with their mother. In her house, they each had their own room and a closet full of new clothes. Vivian Baxter gave them everything they needed. She made sure they went to school and did their homework. Both were excellent students and even skipped a grade after moving to St. Louis.

Vivian worked in taverns and in gambling businesses, so she was never home at night. But Maya and Bailey were not alone. Vivian's boyfriend, Mr. Freeman, also lived in the house. He looked after them when Vivian was out.

Betrayal

Mr. Freeman was a quiet, older man. He didn't do much, and he often spent his evenings just waiting for Vivian to come home. But shortly after Maya and Bailey moved in, Mr. Freeman began doing things that were wrong.

He began touching Maya. At first, the eight-year-old little girl enjoyed being held in his lap. She had never really known her own father, so she liked the attention she got from Mr. Freeman. She was so young that she didn't suspect he was doing anything wrong.

But then one day, Mr. Freeman hurt Maya. He touched her roughly and then he forced himself on her. Her mother's boyfriend raped Maya. It was painful and frightening, and Maya wondered if she would live through it. Then Mr. Freeman threatened Maya. He said that if she told anyone what he had done, he would kill Bailey. Maya loved her brother very much, so she was terrified.

That day when Vivian came home, Maya was in bed. Vivian thought her daughter was sick, so she tried to take care of her. Maya was afraid to tell anyone what Mr. Freeman had done to her. But Vivian soon realized what had happened. She took Maya to the hospital, and she told Mr. Freeman to get out of her house.

In the hospital, Maya received flowers and visits from all of her family. Everyone tried to make her feel better. Maya was healing physically, but inside she felt very sad.

In Court

Mr. Freeman was arrested, and in court Maya had to tell what he had done to her. She knew she had to be brave and tell the truth. After a series of questions, one lawyer then asked her, "Did the accused touch you before the occasion on which you claimed he raped you?"

Maya thought of the times Mr. Freeman had held her in his lap. She thought of the times she had believed that she had liked his touch. And suddenly she was scared.

"No," she replied. She was afraid to tell the truth. She was afraid to say that—for a little while—she thought that this man had loved her.

Mr. Freeman was convicted of rape and sentenced to a term in prison. But somehow his lawyers got him released the same afternoon.

Later that night though, Mr. Freeman was found—kicked to death. Maya had a feeling that her uncles had taken matters into their own hands.

Silence

When Maya heard about Mr. Freeman's murder, she felt terrible. She began to think that everything was her fault. She worried that she had done something to deserve the pain he had caused her. And she worried that her words had caused Mr. Freeman to die.

In her mind, Maya believed that her voice had caused a man to die. She couldn't understand that it was the man's own actions that had gotten him in trouble. She remembered thinking:

A man was dead because I lied. . . . I could feel the evilness flowing through my body and waiting, pent up, to rush off my tongue if I tried to open my mouth. I clamped by teeth shut, I'd hold it in.

Soon she began just to listen to everything around her. Sounds hummed in her ears, and she decided not to speak. Her family did not understand what was wrong with her. They thought she should get over what had happened. They felt her silence was rude, and often she was punished for not speaking.

The family in St. Louis did not know how to deal with Maya. So, before long, Maya and Bailey were sent back to Arkansas. Maybe Momma could help her. Bailey cried as the train pulled out of St. Louis. But Maya just listened and said nothing.

FINDING A VOICE

FOR ALMOST A YEAR, Maya spoke to no one except Bailey. She went to school and did her homework, but she never talked in class. And she never talked to Momma. She kept her words to herself.

During this time, Maya began to write. She kept journals and she wrote poetry. She also began to read everything she could. She discovered the works of William Shakespeare and Charles Dickens. And she also began to read books by African-American writers such as Langston Hughes, Paul Laurence Dunbar, and James Weldon Johnson.

Langston Hughes, one of the many African-American writers whom Maya came to respect and admire

This was a very lonely time for young Maya. She seemed to withdraw farther and farther into her own separate world.

A Lifeline

Then one afternoon while she was working in the Store, Maya had another change in her life. As she explained later, "For nearly a year, I sopped around the house, the Store, the school and the church, like an old biscuit, dirty and inedible. Then I met, or rather got to know, the lady who threw me my first lifeline."

That lady was Mrs. Bertha Flowers, the richest black woman in Stamps. Mrs. Flowers dressed well and spoke perfect English. Maya never saw her laugh, but Mrs. Flowers always gave her a kind smile.

And on that particular afternoon, Mrs. Flowers invited Maya to her home. Momma agreed that she could go, so Maya changed her dress and left the Store. As she and Mrs. Flowers walked along the road, the woman spoke to Maya. She said that she had heard what a bright girl Maya was. But she had also heard that Maya would not talk at school or anywhere else. Mrs. Flowers spoke about how important language was. She told Maya that words were not meant only to be written or read. They were meant to be spoken. Maya said nothing, but she listened to all that the woman said.

At Mrs. Flowers' home, Maya was given lemonade and cookies. Maya couldn't believe all the attention she was getting. She loved having someone spend time with her the way Mrs. Flowers was.

Then Mrs. Flowers picked up a book, Charles Dickens's *A Tale of Two Cities*, and she began to read aloud. Maya listened to the woman's beautiful voice. When Mrs. Flowers stopped reading, she asked Maya if she liked what was being read. "Yes, ma'am," Maya answered. Her silence was broken.

Later, Mrs. Flowers told Maya she could borrow any of her books, as long as she returned them in good condition. Maya was thrilled by this new library that had been given to her. Mrs. Flowers then told Maya to take a book of poems and to memorize one of the poems for their next visit.

As she left Mrs. Flowers' home that day—only to return many times after—Maya realized something very important. She realized that she mattered, that she was an important person to this woman. It was the first step toward knowing that she was an important person in the world. As Maya Angelou later wrote, "I was liked, and what a difference it made. I was respected not as Mrs. Henderson's grandchild or Bailey's sister but for just being Marguerite Johnson."

Moving On

In the spring of 1940, Maya graduated from the eighth grade. She was an honor student, and she was looking forward to high school. Life had become much better for Maya during recent years, and she felt she had much to look forward to.

But then one day, things changed again. Bailey came home and said he had seen white men taking the body of a black man out of a river. Momma knew that the man had been lynched—killed by a group of white men. Bailey looked scared, and Momma knew he was no longer safe in Stamps.

By that time, Vivian Baxter had married again and had moved to San Francisco. It was decided that Maya and Bailey would go to live with her. Vivian's

Many African-American men were lynched by groups of white men in the South.

new husband was a successful businessman. Maya and Bailey called him Daddy Clidell, and he turned out to be a good stepfather.

In San Francisco

Maya loved the sights and sounds of the new city. She found San Francisco to be a wonderfully stimulating place. She went to George Washington High School, which was in a white part of town. Maya was one of only three black students there. She was self-conscious about being in that school, but one of her teachers—Miss Kirwin—made her feel more at ease.

Miss Kirwin taught civics and current events. She encouraged her students to learn about the world around them. And she treated all of her students with respect. She didn't treat blacks any differently from the way she treated whites. Miss Kirwin made Maya feel like an intelligent young woman.

In high school, Maya won a scholarship from a local college. That scholarship allowed her to take night classes in drama and dancing. She enjoyed learning about acting, and she loved dancing in her

Maya found San Francisco to be a wonderful and exciting place. She enjoyed the city and took classes in drama and dancing.

black tights. For a short while, life in San Francisco seemed very good to Maya.

Summer in Los Angeles

When Maya was fifteen, her father invited her to spend the summer with him in Los Angeles. Maya was thrilled. She had visions of the tropical paradise in which her father lived, and she couldn't wait to get there.

Dolores Stockland, her father's new girlfriend, met Maya at the train station, and Maya wondered what this summer would hold for her. But before long, Maya's excitement was crushed. Dolores was very young, and she did not like the idea of her boyfriend's daughter getting in the way. Also, Bailey Sr. lived in a run-down trailer park.

Maya tried to make the most of the summer, but there was a great deal of tension between her and Dolores. It only grew worse when Bailey Sr. invited Maya to go with him on a car trip to Mexico one day. Dolores felt left out and did not like it.

The trip to Mexico proved to be an adventure, however. Once in Mexico, her father got drunk and couldn't drive. So Maya found herself driving his car out of Mexico. When she had a minor accident at the border, her father woke up and fin-

When Maya went to visit her father in California, she expected palm trees and paradise. What she encountered was quite different.

ished the drive back to Los Angeles. Maya had never driven before, so the trip was both exciting and terrifying.

When they got back to the trailer, Maya and Dolores had a terrible argument. Dolores became very angry and attacked Maya. She felt that Maya was coming between her and her boyfriend. At that point, Bailey Sr. knew he had to get Maya out of that home. He sent her to stay with friends for a while, but Maya grew restless. She didn't know where her father was or when he was coming back. So one day, she just left the friends' home and began walking around Los Angeles. She spent the night in a car in a junkyard.

The next morning, she met a whole community of teenagers who lived in the junkyard. They welcomed her to their "neighborhood," and she quickly became a part of it. She lived with the group and learned how to survive on the street. But finally, after a month of living in the junkyard, she called her mother and said it was time to go home. Vivian Baxter sent Maya a plane ticket, and soon she was headed back to San Francisco.

Though it was a dangerous summer for her, Maya had fond memories of her time in the junkyard. The other kids there had immediately accepted her, and for once she had felt as though she belonged.

Growing Up

In the following months, when Bailey was about sixteen years old, he began to pull away from the family. He stayed out late and wanted to be more independent. Before long, he moved out. Maya was devastated. Bailey had always been her closest companion, and she knew she would miss him.

Maya decided she needed a change too. After much thought, she decided to take a semester off school and get a job. She wanted a job as a conductor on a San Francisco cable car. At this time, during World War II (1939–1945), many women worked as conductors because the men were fighting overseas. But there had never been a black woman conductor.

Maya's mother supported her daughter's idea but warned her it might not be easy. First, Maya filled out an application for the job, but she was not given an interview. She knew her race was a factor, but she decided not to give up. Every day, she went down to the office and waited. For several days, she was ignored. But finally, someone gave in. Maya's

During World War II, Maya became the first African-American woman to work as the conductor of a San Francisco cable car.

persistence paid off, and she was given the job. She was San Francisco's first black woman cable-car conductor!

For a semester, Maya enjoyed her job and her independence. She got to see the city each day, and she had money to spend. When she went back to school, her attitude had changed. The other kids seemed immature to her, and she couldn't really focus on schoolwork. She was ready for the real world.

Real Adulthood

As Maya finished her last year in high school in 1945, she began to think of herself as a young woman. She had never dated, and she did not think she was pretty. She began to worry that maybe no one would ever be interested in her.

At that point, she began to pursue a boy who lived nearby. She was curious, and she wanted to find out more about relationships. The boy was responsive to her, and soon they spent the night together.

That experience was not very special, but Maya felt she knew more about herself. What she did not know—until a few weeks later—was that she was pregnant.

When Maya realized she was carrying a child, she was terribly afraid. She decided not to tell anyone. She felt as though she would bring shame to the family. For months and months, Maya kept her secret to herself. Then, on the night she graduated from high school, she left her mother and Daddy Clidell a note about the pregnancy.

I am sorry to bring this disgrace on the family, but I am pregnant.

Marguerite

At first, Maya's mother and Daddy Clidell were shocked about Maya's pregnancy. But then they became very supportive. They took care of Maya and insisted that she and the baby live with them. So, shortly after she graduated from high school, Maya became a mother. She gave birth to a little boy and named him Clyde Bailey Johnson.

AFRICAN
HERITAGES

4

OR THE NEXT seven years, Maya did all she could to support her young son. She worked at a series of jobs and even moved back to Stamps, Arkansas, for a while. But it was in San Francisco that Maya met her first husband.

Marriage

Maya loved shopping at a store called Melrose Records. She and the owner, Louise Cox, became friendly. At one point Louise introduced Maya to R.L. Poole, a jazz tap dancer from Chicago. Maya was eager to learn more about dance, and Poole liked her enthusiasm. He taught her all that he could.

Then Louise gave Maya a job at Melrose Records. Maya was touched by how nice this white woman was being toward her. She began to realize that some white people treat black people as equals.

While she was working at the record store, Maya met Tosh Angelos. He was a white man, a sailor who loved jazz music as much as she did. Tosh was very kind to her, and he enjoyed spending time with young Clyde as well. In 1952, Maya and Tosh were married.

For a while, Maya was very happy. She was able to be a full-time mother and wife. And she had time for more dance lessons too. But soon, the differences between Maya and her husband caused problems. She had always been very religious, but Tosh did not believe in God. He did not like it when Maya went to church. And he wanted Maya to forget about her family and where she came from.

Soon Maya realized she had made a mistake. She felt that her husband was trying to change her or make her into something she wasn't. Before long, she and Tosh got a divorce.

A Dancing Life

After her marriage was over, Maya got jobs singing and dancing in local clubs in San Francisco. Audiences enjoyed her performances, and many felt she had a certain presence on stage.

At one point, she worked as a singer in a club called the Purple Onion. She had been using Rita (short for Marguerite) Johnson as her stage name. But the manager at the Purple Onion thought she needed a more interesting name. He liked the name Maya, the nickname her brother had given her. And he heard of her former husband's last name, Angelos. Someone suggested that she change her last name to "Angelou," and that's how she became known as Maya Angelou.

Her act at the Purple Onion was a favorite with many of the regulars. She loved her job and the people she met. Soon her circle of friends included painters, writers, and musicians. These creative people added so much to Angelou's outlook on the world. They made her think differently and look at herself in a new way. She continued to write poetry as she had done years before. And soon she began to set the words of her poetry to music.

The Purple Onion in San Francisco. It was here that the stage name Maya Angelou was created.

Off to Europe

During this time in her life, Angelou also began going to operas and musicals. She was thrilled by the big productions, especially *Porgy and Bess*. This opera, written by George Gershwin, is set in the southern United States. Over the years, it has become a classic.

A scene from Porgy and Bess. *Angelou performed in European and African tours of this show.*

In 1954, Angelou was offered a starring role in the European and African tour of *Porgy and Bess*. It would play in twenty-two countries. Members of the American tour had seen Angelou at the Purple Onion, and she had made a good impression. Angelou couldn't believe the opportunity she was given.

The only problem she faced was what to do with her son. Clyde could not accompany her on such a long tour. Luckily, Angelou's mother stepped in and offered to take care of her grandson while Angelou was away.

Maya Angelou first went to Montreal, Canada, where the group began rehearsals. She enjoyed learning the words to the musical and performing the dance routines. On stage, Angelou felt truly alive.

After that time in Canada, Angelou and the troupe left for Italy. They were overwhelmed by the welcome they received in Venice. Crowds of people met their bus, and audiences loved the show. Angelou remembered:

The opening night of our European tour was a smash hit. The Italians were the most difficult audiences to sing for. They knew and loved music; operas, which were mainly for the elite in other countries, were folk music and children's songs in Italy. They loved us, we loved them. We loved ourselves. It was a certainty; if Italy declared us acceptable we could have the rest of Europe for a song.

The next stop was Paris. The French audiences supported the opera enthusiastically, so the troupe extended their performances there for several months. While in Paris, Angelou met many African-Americans who had moved to France. They found the European atmosphere much more welcoming than the United States had been for them. For a time, Angelou considered staying in Paris, but finally she decided to continue with the tour.

The opera troupe eventually made its way to Cairo, Egypt. In Egypt, Angelou felt immediately at home. Many important people in Cairo had skin as dark as Angelou's. For once, she was not in the minority.

While in Egypt, Angelou began to think about her African heritage. She did not know where her ancestors came from, but she thought about them as she explored the ancient country.

The troupe then continued to Athens, Tel Aviv, Milan, and Rome. But then Angelou got a message that her son Clyde was sick. She left the opera and immediately went back to San Francisco as quickly as she could.

Reunited

By the time Angelou saw Clyde again, she had been away for a year. She had missed her son terribly but had no idea how her absence had affected him. He was sickly and frail, and he just wanted to stay in her lap and be held by her. Angelou remembered when she first saw Clyde after her return:

> Clyde had little to say. The . . . beautiful and bubbling child I had left had disappeared. In his place was a rough-skinned, shy boy who hung his head when spoken to and refused to maintain eye contact even when I held his chin and asked, "Look at me."

Angelou knew that Clyde needed her complete attention. She made him all his favorite meals, and she took him on many walks and picnics. She spent as much time with him as she could, and she listened to all his ideas. She knew she had been gone far too long, and she vowed not to have such a separation from her son again.

Before long, Clyde's health improved. And then he made an important announcement. He had decided that he did not like his name and wanted to change it. From then on, he wished to be called "Guy." At first, Angelou didn't know what to think about this change. But soon she began calling her son Guy, just as he had requested.

More Changes

For a while, Angelou stayed close to home. She sang in nightclubs and did all she could to support herself and her son. In 1957, she and Guy moved to New York City.

There, Angelou found another singing job. But before long, she wanted to try something new. She didn't believe that she had what it took to be a great singer, and she wanted to do something important with her life. Angelou was beginning to realize that she had something to say and she needed to find a way to say it.

Angelou and her son moved to New York City in 1957. The cultural atmosphere was inspiring to the up-and-coming writer.

Becoming a Writer

Maya Angelou had been keeping journals and writing poetry for years, but she had never pursued writing as a career. In the 1950s, African-Americans were becoming more prominent as writers and playwrights. Angelou enjoyed the works of Lorraine Hansberry and James Baldwin. She began to consider putting her own thoughts on paper.

Lorraine Hansberry, a prominent African-American writer during the 1950s, was an inspiration for Maya Angelou.

At the urging of a friend, Angelou joined the Harlem Writers Guild. This group of African-American writers met in members' homes. They read their writing to one another and offered criticism and advice. In the beginning, Angelou just listened to the works of others, but soon she began to read her own writing aloud. At first, she found criticism from the others hard to take. But eventually she was able to consider their comments with an open mind. Their encouragement helped her to work hard at her writing.

James Baldwin, author of Go Tell It on the Mountain. *His work had an impact on Angelou.*

The Civil Rights Movement

At about this time, the civil rights movement was growing throughout the United States. Black citizens in the South were beginning to question their separation from whites. They began to demand the same rights as whites.

In response to these issues, the Southern Christian Leadership Conference (SCLC) was formed, with Dr. Martin Luther King Jr. as its leader. The SCLC worked to gain racial equality, and Angelou supported its efforts.

The SCLC questioned the separation of blacks and whites. Angelou supported their demonstrations.

One day, she and a friend named Godfrey Cambridge went to hear Martin Luther King Jr. speak at a local Harlem church. He was an amazing speaker, and he often had a great effect on his audiences. Angelou later remembered that he was "a magnificent spirit . . . a great spiritual leader and an extraordinary man."

Both Angelou and Cambridge were inspired by him, and they wanted to help his cause. So, with the permission of the SCLC, Angelou and Cambridge decided to write and produce a musical revue called *Cabaret for Freedom.*

The show was a huge success and raised a great deal of money for the SCLC. Dr. King was especially impressed with the work Angelou had done, and he quickly offered her a job as the northern coordinator for the SCLC. She was honored to be asked and accepted the position.

In her role for the SCLC, Angelou organized student volunteers and worked with them to raise money for the group. As part of the campaign, she sent out thousands of letters and made hundreds of phone calls. It was hard work, but she knew that the work was important.

Dr. Martin Luther King Jr. was a key figure in the civil rights movement. Angelou supported his efforts.

Another Chance at Love

One night in 1961, at a civil rights meeting in Harlem, Angelou met a very interesting man. He was Vusumzi Make, a freedom fighter from South Africa. He had come to the United States to tell people about the racial problems in his own country. At that time in South Africa, a system called apartheid ruled the country. Apartheid separated the black people from the white people. Blacks could not attend good schools or live in white neighborhoods. And they could not hold public office, even though there were many more blacks than whites in South Africa.

Angelou was inspired by Vusumzi Make's words. She admired his courage, and she respected the work he was doing. They felt a connection through their work, and they were immediately attracted to each other. Within a matter of days, Maya and Vusumzi were married.

For a time, Maya, her son Guy, and Vusumzi remained in New York. Vusumzi continued his work at the United Nations, and Maya starred in a play called *The Blacks* by Jean Genet. But before long, the new family decided to move to Egypt. A very exciting part of Maya's life was just beginning.

Under the system of apartheid, South Africa's blacks and whites were strictly separated.

In Egypt

Maya Angelou and her son found Cairo, Egypt, to be a busy and beautiful city, and they loved their time there. They enjoyed walking the streets and shopping in the markets. Their home was nicely furnished, and they met many interesting people.

But quite soon, things within the marriage became difficult. Vusumzi Make expected Maya to stay home and be a housewife. But Maya wanted to do her own work, and she did not like to be told what to do. Soon she took a job as a writer for *The Arab Observer.*

Vusumzi did not approve of Maya's new job, however. He began to travel more, and the two began to drift apart. Before long, Maya's second marriage was over.

At Home in Africa

Even though Maya Angelou and Vusumzi Make chose to divorce, Angelou wanted to stay in Africa. Guy had decided to attend the University of Ghana, and Maya felt she could make the continent of Africa her new home.

When Guy started college in 1963, Angelou accompanied him to Accra, Ghana's capital city. She

A marketplace in Accra. Angelou accompanied her son to this city in Ghana when he went to college.

enjoyed exploring Accra and learning about its people. She liked being among other black people, and she felt really at home there.

She also began working for *The Ghanian Times*. The pace at the paper was quick and frantic. She described her first visit there: "The editor's office . . . had all the excitement of a busy city intersection. People came, left, talked, shouted, laid down papers, picked up packages, spoke English, Fanti, Twi, Ga, and Pidgin on the telephone or to each other."

On weekends, Angelou roamed around the countryside of Ghana. She saw the prisons where slaves had been held many years before as they waited to be shipped to the American colonies. She wondered if her own ancestors had been kept in those very same prisons.

At one point, Angelou had another personal challenge to handle. Guy was in a terrible car accident, and he remained in the hospital for quite a while. For a time, nobody knew if Guy would live or not. Angelou took care of him as best she could, and she was very grateful when he recovered from his injuries.

Angelou enjoyed the many people she met in Ghana. She liked speaking with the African people, and she began wearing African clothes. Soon she learned to cook African meals, and she learned to speak several African languages. She remembered, "The music of the Fanti language was becoming singable to me, and its vocabulary was moving orderly through my brain."

Continuing the Work for Civil Rights

During her time in Ghana, Angelou also enjoyed the company of the other black Americans she met there. Hundreds of African-Americans had come to Ghana to live. Among them were Julian Mayfield, a friend of Angelou's from the Harlem Writers Guild, and the famous writer W.E.B. Du Bois.

These creative people did much to encourage Angelou. She began to see her writing as art, and she tried to nurture the talent she had. Years later, she wrote, "We need art to live fully and to grow healthily. Without art, we are dry husks drifting aimlessly on every ill wind; our fortunes are without promise and our present without grace."

One day, while visiting Julian Mayfield, Angelou was introduced to Malcolm X. He was a civil rights leader who was doing important work in the United States. Malcolm X came to believe that violence was not the answer to the racial problems America faced. Instead, he felt that progress could be made through peaceful protests and discussions. Angelou

Malcolm X, a prominent civil rights leader. Angelou met him and was moved by his ideas.

agreed with him and was quite moved by her conversation with him.

Shortly after Malcolm X returned to the United States, he wrote to Angelou. He asked her to come back and work for him in the Organization for Afro-American Unity. Angelou thought very hard about his proposal. She loved living in Ghana and felt a strong connection to its people. But she also knew that the civil rights movement was important. She decided it was time to return to the United States and get to work.

A Connection in Keta

Before Angelou left Ghana, she visited the small village of Keta. As she strolled through the streets, Angelou met a woman whose appearance startled her. The tall, strong woman looked so much like Momma Henderson! And the woman seemed to think Angelou looked familiar too.

Soon many of the villagers agreed that Angelou looked like one of them. So they told her the story of their village. Many years before, most of the people in the village were kidnapped and sold into slavery. Whole families were taken, and the village was burned down. Only a few children escaped. Years later, these children returned to the village as adults and rebuilt it.

It made Angelou sad to think that her own relatives may have been captured and forced into slavery in that very village. But at the same time, Angelou was happy to think that she had found her roots. Her history made more sense to her, and she felt a very special connection to the people of Keta. Later, as she stood at the airport preparing to return to the United States, Angelou realized that:

I knew my people had never completely left Africa. We had sung it in our blues, shouted it in our gospel and danced the continent in our breakdowns. As we carried [Africa] to Philadelphia, Boston and Birmingham we had changed its color, modified its rhythms, yet it was Africa which rode in the bulges of our high calves, shook in our protruding behinds and crackled in our wide open laughter.

POETRY AND FAME

SOON AFTER MAYA returned to the United States, Malcolm X was assassinated. His death was followed a few years later by the assassination of Martin Luther King Jr. It was a difficult time for the civil rights movement in the United States. Riots broke out throughout the country. It was definitely a time of uncertainty.

Angelou was devastated by the loss of Malcolm X and Martin Luther King Jr., but she knew her own work had to continue. She began to draw on her own experiences in order to inspire others. She remembered what Malcolm X had once told her: "You have seen African, bring it home and teach our people about the homeland."

Through her writing, Angelou soon became an important voice for all Americans.

Finding Fame

In 1968, Maya Angelou wrote and narrated a ten-part program for National Public Radio. This series of successful programs was called *Maya Angelou's America: A Journey of the Heart*, and her son Guy Johnson produced it.

In 1969, Angelou wrote *I Know Why the Caged Bird Sings*. The book deals with Angelou's early life, describing her childhood in Arkansas, St. Louis, and California. Critics praised this work as honest, touching, and heroic. James Baldwin said, "This testimony from a black sister marks the beginning of a new era in the mind and hearts and lives of all black men and women. . . ."

I Know Why the Caged Bird Sings is probably Angelou's best-known work. Her chronicle of her own childhood and her difficult beginnings spoke to many people, both black and white. It hit the bestseller list and sold many copies. In 1970, the book was nominated for a National Book Award, and years later, it was made into a two-hour television movie.

In an interview with David Frost, Angelou spoke of the importance of this book to her. And she talked about its memorable title. She explained that she had taken the now-famous title from the lines of a poem called "Sympathy," written by the famous and influential African-American poet Paul Laurence Dunbar.

I know why the caged bird sings, ah me,
  When his wing is bruised and his bosom sore, —
When he beats his bars and he would be free;
It is not a carol of joy or glee,
  But a prayer that he sends from his heart's deep core,
But a plea, that upward to Heaven he flings—
I know why the caged bird sings!

For many years of her life, Angelou herself had been a caged bird. But she never gave up. Her song was a prayer of hope, and she found her own amazing voice.

With a copy of I Know Why the Caged Bird Sings. *This auto-biographical work was nominated for a National Book Award.*

A Published Poet

In 1971, Maya Angelou published her first volume of poetry, *Just Give Me a Cool Drink of Water 'fore I Diiie*. Four years later *Oh, Pray My Wings Are Gonna Fit Me Well*, her second book of poetry, was published. Other volumes—including *Shaker, Why Don't You Sing?*; *And Still I Rise*; and *I Shall Not Be Moved*—followed over the years.

Another Try at Marriage

In 1973, Angelou married Paul de Feu, an English writer and cartoonist. For much of the 1970s, they resided in northern California and had a wonderful life together. They enjoyed cooking and entertaining. And often their home was filled with family and friends. It was also during this time that her grandson, Colin Ashanti Murphy-Johnson, was born.

Working on Big and Small Screens

In 1976, Angelou appeared in the television miniseries *Roots*. This work, based on the book by Alex Haley, was a national phenomenon. It traced the roots of an African slave named Kunte Kinte. Angelou received an Emmy Award nomination for her role as Kunte Kinte's grandmother.

Other television work included guest appearances on *Touched by an Angel, Sesame Street,* and *Moesha.* She wrote for Oprah Winfrey's series *Brewster Place,* and she also wrote six one-half-hour programs for *Assignment America.*

Angelou appeared in the 1996 film *Elmo Saves Christmas.* She was featured in *How to Make an American Quilt,* a 1995 film directed by Jocelyn Moorhouse. And she narrated the 1995 film, *The Journey of August King,* which starred Jason Patric and Thandie Newton.

In 1972, Angelou wrote the screenplay for *Georgia, Georgia,* the story of a young black American singer living in Stockholm. This screenplay was the first one written by a black woman ever to be filmed. She wrote the screenplay for the television movie based on her book *I Know Why the Caged Bird Sings.* This 1979 movie starred Diahann Carroll and Paul Benjamin. She also wrote and produced *Three Way Choice,* a miniseries for CBS.

Angelou has written and produced a number of film documentaries. In 1968, she wrote, produced, and directed *Black, Blues, Black.* This was a series of ten one-hour programs for National Education Television.

On the set of Down in the Delta. *Angelou directed and produced this 1999 feature film.*

She won the Golden Eagle Award in 1977 for *Afro-Americans in the Arts*, a special she created for PBS. She also worked on a number of other documentary projects for PBS including *Who Cares About Kids, Kindred Spirits*, and *Maya Angelou: Rainbow in the Clouds*.

Maya Angelou's poems are a vital part of the talented African-American filmmaker John Singleton's 1993 film, *Poetic Justice*. This movie starred Janet Jackson as a young writer.

Down in the Delta is a 1999 feature film that Angelou directed. The movie stars Alfre Woodard as a young woman who goes to live with relatives in rural Mississippi. The film, which touches on issues of family, race, and history, also stars Esther Rolle and Wesley Snipes.

Writing More about Herself

Gather Together in My Name, the second of Angelou's autobiographical works was published in 1986 and chronicles her life in Ghana. In this book, Angelou describes the African continent and her connection to it. And she talks about a longing: "The ache for home which lives in all of us, the place where we can go as we are."

Maya Angelou's Message

Like many writers, Maya Angelou has had great success in writing about what she knows. Her own childhood provided the basis for her first book. And her subsequent work has relied heavily on her own life experiences.

Angelou's poetry is inspired by her thoughts and feelings about the world around her. Her work reflects her bad experiences, such as the racism and abuse she suffered, as well as her hope for the human race. The writing of Maya Angelou is very much a part of her soul.

Awards and Honors

As Angelou continued to publish her poetry and write her autobiographies, she received many honors. In 1975, President Gerald Ford appointed her to the American Revolution Bicentennial Council. Also in 1975, Angelou was named Woman of the Year by *Ladies Home Journal* magazine. And two years later, President Jimmy Carter asked her to join the National Commission on the Observance of International Women's Year. Angelou's *Give Me a Cool Drink of Water 'Fore I Diiie* was nominated for a Pulitzer Prize in poetry.

*Honoring the 1976 Ladies Home Journal Woman of the Year,
Betty Ford (third from right). Angelou (third from left) won the
award the previous year.*

In 1975, she was named to the board of trustees
for the American Film Institute, and she currently is
a member of the Director's Guild of America. In
1983, she received the Matrix Award, an honor from
Women in Communications, Inc. In 1992, Angelou
was named Woman of the Year by *Essence* magazine.
That same year, she received the Horatio Alger
Award. In 1991, she won the Langston Hughes
Award from the City College of New York.

At the 1994 Grammy Awards ceremony. Angelou received an award for best spoken word performance.

Angelou has received numerous honorary degrees and has received awards for her work in the civil rights movement. She was named to the New York Black 100 by the Schomberg Center in Harlem, and she received an award from the Tubman African American Museum in Macon, Georgia.

In 1982, Angelou was named the Reynolds Professor of American Studies at Wake Forest Univer-

Angelou with Senator Edward Kennedy and two other winners of the 1983 Matrix Award for excellence in communications

sity in Winston-Salem, North Carolina. She still holds this post and lives today in that college town.

As a Mother

Over the years, Angelou made great efforts to include her son in her life. Her separation from him during her time on the *Porgy and Bess* tour had been very difficult for her. In her later writings, she revealed that her guilt about being away from him nearly led her to suicide.

Having a child must have been a hard thing for Angelou. She was very young and unmarried when she discovered she was pregnant, but she did the best she could to be a good mother. Guy Johnson has learned much from his famous mother, and he has made a life for himself. Once he explained, "Many people whose parents are mountains feel overshadowed, hemmed in. I feel liberated. She has shown me what is possible with perseverance. I too can construct my own mountain, and I can start building on top of hers."

A REMARKABLE JOURNEY

O N A COLD January day in 1993, Maya Angelou stood on the steps of the Capitol in Washington, D.C., at the inauguration of President Bill Clinton. She looked out at the large crowd of people before her. Television cameras focused on her, and microphones waited for her to begin. And when she spoke, the whole world listened.

Shortly after President Clinton was elected in November 1992, he called Angelou and asked her to write a poem for his inauguration. She got right to work. And she knew that this poem had to be special.

Delivering her poem "On the Pulse of the Morning" at President Bill Clinton's inauguration in 1993

She called the poem "On the Pulse of the Morning." It spoke about a new beginning for the United States. The poem asks people of all races and beliefs to have courage—courage to face the past and courage to hope for the future.

When the time came for her to deliver the poem, Angelou walked up the long red carpet to the podium. She braced herself against the chilling wind and kept her coat pulled tightly around her. As she prepared to speak, she may have thought about her humble beginnings. And she may have marveled at how far she had come.

Years of Thought

In the years since Angelou delivered her famous poem at President Clinton's inauguration, she has continued to write and influence those around her.

In 1995, she published *A Brave and Startling Truth*, a poem she wrote and delivered at the celebration of the fiftieth anniversary of the United Nations. That same year, she published *Phenomenal Woman*, a book containing four poems that honor women.

Also in 1995, Maya Angelou spoke at the Million Man March in Washington, D.C. This gathering was

Speaking at the Million Man March on October 16, 1995, in Washington, D.C. Angelou delivered her poem "From a Black Woman to a Black Man."

a forum for African-American men to meet and make a commitment to their roles in their families and communities. Angelou wrote the poem "From a Black Woman to a Black Man" and delivered it at the event.

Maya Angelou has also written books for children. She teamed up with photographer Margaret Courtney-Clarke to produce *My Painted House, My Friendly Chicken, and Me* in 1994. Two years later, they published *Kofi and His Magic*. Then in 1998, Angelou published *Life Doesn't Frighten Me*, a picture book that can be appreciated by readers of all ages.

In 1993, she published *Wouldn't Take Nothing for My Journey Now*, a collection of essays. Four years later, she followed it with *Even the Stars Look Lonesome*. In these books, Angelou reflects on all she has learned in her life. She talks about relationships— her marriages and her third divorce in 1981—as well as motherhood, friendship, and virtues.

Regarding the virtues she holds dear, Angelou says:

We must replace fear and chauvinism, hate timidity and apathy, which flow in our national

spinal column, with courage, sensitivity, perse-
verance and, I even dare say "love." And by "love"
I mean that condition in the human spirit so
profound it encourages us to develop courage. It
is said that courage is the most important of all
virtues, because without courage you can't prac-
tice any other virtue consistently.

Continuing Causes

Even as Angelou grows older, she continues to work for the causes she believes in. In 1996, she was appointed as a national ambassador for the United Nations International Children's Emergency Fund (UNICEF). This organization raises money to help children all over the world. She also supports the United Negro College Fund and appeared in a promotional piece for that group.

Helping children is important to Maya Angelou. She remembers that as a child reading helped her get through some difficult times. So she has worked to improve literacy throughout the world. It is her hope that everyone will learn to read. She believes that reading can give hope to people from all backgrounds.

Angelou doesn't shy away from the difficult

Over the years, Angelou has touched the world through books, films, television, and theater.

Cooking for a charity benefit in New York City. Angelou's talents are not limited to the written word.

causes either. The South African apartheid she learned about in the 1960s continued to exist until the early 1990s. In 1988, she and Alice Walker—a friend and fellow writer—attended an anti-apartheid demonstration in Berkeley, California. They were both arrested during the demonstration. But Angelou has this memory of the African-American police officer who arrested her, "Her hands were shaking, and she asked me for my autograph."

Remembering Her Heritage

Some days, Angelou dresses in stylish and conservative clothing. But other days, she enjoys wearing African dresses and headwraps. These items in her wardrobe remind her of her own heritage and of the time she spent on the African continent.

Her home is decorated with African statues and carvings. And on the walls are paintings by noted African-American artists. Often African music fills the rooms of her home as she entertains family and friends.

On Religion

The religious upbringing that Angelou experienced had a profound impact on the rest of her life. Even when she found herself in difficult circumstances, she retained her faith in God. She knew that the strength Momma had helped to instill in her would always sustain her. And even when she was alone, she knew that strength remained. In *Even the Stars Look Lonesome*, Angelou writes:

> It is in the interludes between being in company that we talk to ourselves. In the silence we listen to ourselves. Then we ask questions of ourselves. We describe ourselves to ourselves, and in the quietude we may even hear the voice of God.

Influence

Maya Angelou's words have affected many people throughout the world. Her books have reached millions of readers of all races and ages.

One person who read Angelou's work and later became her friend is Oprah Winfrey. Winfrey could relate to Angelou's difficult childhood. She too had known racism, and she too had been the victim of sexual abuse. When Winfrey later interviewed Angelou, it was as though she was meeting her idol.

Oprah Winfrey is one of the many celebrities Angelou has influenced; the two women have developed a special friendship.

Since that initial meeting, Angelou and Winfrey have developed a very special friendship. Winfrey calls Angelou her Mother-Sister-Friend. But Winfrey knows that she shares her friend with the world: "She is a constant force of inspiration. I know she's always ready for whatever is needed. Her great gift to all who love her is that each of us feels most loved by her."

In Person

In addition to being an accomplished writer and filmmaker, Maya Angelou has also become an important public speaker. For a time, she was making as many as eighty appearances a year. She lectures usually to packed houses, and she has developed quite a following. Some have even described her speeches as "hypnotic."

Her students at Wake Forest University would probably agree. There she has the freedom to teach all sorts of classes in the humanities. And she enjoys sharing what she knows with her students. However, she explains what she feels her role really is.

The teacher doesn't teach, not really. The teacher offers stimulation and ways in which the person can educate himself or herself. At best the teacher wakes up, shakes that person and makes a person hungry.

Always a Writer

No matter how busy her days are, Angelou remains a writer first. She sticks to a schedule and insists on writing every day. During the 1970s, when she was producing the most, Angelou would sometimes write for sixteen hours a day. More recently, she usually writes in the morning and tends to other matters in the afternoon. Then she leaves herself time in the evenings to edit her writing. She still refers to writing as the most important and fulfilling part of her life.

To the Top of the Mountain

While Angelou can be proud of the influence her words have had on the people of the world, she can take special joy in the relationship she has developed with her son, Guy. When fame enters a person's life, that person's family often feels left out, or left behind. But as he has matured, Guy has found happiness as part of his mother's life. His words may well be the greatest compliment to her accomplishments:

Just as Angelou was inspired by others, she has proven to be an inspiration to millions.

I was raised as an only child, but because of my
mother I have many brothers and sisters. I share
her easily because one cannot own the dew, the
snow, the wind, the rain. It is a force of nature.
It took no talent to be her son, and I don't see her
success as mine. However, her accomplishments
lead like stairs to the top of a mountain, and I
feel free to climb them.

No doubt, Maya Angelou has served as the stairs for many people as they have begun to climb a mountain. Her work for human rights has encouraged people throughout the world. And her words have helped all kinds of people to do their best, to treat others well, and ultimately to believe in their own abilities.

TIMELINE

1928   Maya Angelou born Marguerite Annie Johnson on April 4 in St. Louis

1945   Graduates from high school; gives birth to Clyde Bailey Johnson (later known as Guy)

1954   Joins a touring company of *Porgy and Bess*

1957   Moves with Guy to New York; joins the Harlem Writers Guild

1960s   Writes (with Godfrey Cambridge) *Cabaret for Freedom*; begins working with Martin Luther King Jr. as northern coordinator for the Southern Christian Leadership Conference; stars in Jean Genet's *The Blacks*

1961   Moves to Egypt and writes for *The Arab Observer*

1963   Moves to Ghana and writes for *The Ghanian Times*

1965   Returns to the United States

1969   Publishes *I Know Why the Caged Bird Sings*, which is nominated for a National Book Award the next year

1971	Publishes her first book of poetry, *Just Give Me a Cool Drink of Water 'fore I Diiie*
1972	Writes screenplay *Georgia, Georgia*
1974	Publishes *Gather Together in My Name*
1975	Is appointed by President Gerald Ford to American Revolution Bicentennial Council; is named Woman of the Year by *Ladies Home Journal*
1976	Publishes *Singin' and Swingin' and Getting Merry Like Christmas*; writes play *And Still I Rise*; appears in TV miniseries *Roots*
1977	Is appointed by President Jimmy Carter to the National Commission on the Observance of International Women's Year
1981	Publishes *The Heart of a Woman*
1982	Is appointed Reynolds Professor of American Studies at Wake Forest University
1986	Publishes *All God's Children Need Traveling Shoes*
1991	Publishes *I Shall Not Be Moved*
1993	Reads her poem "On the Pulse of the Morning" at the inauguration of President Bill Clinton; publishes *Wouldn't Take Nothing for My Journey Now*
1995	Publishes *A Brave and Startling Truth* and *Phenomenal Woman*
1997	Publishes *Even the Stars Look Lonesome*
1998	Publishes *Life Doesn't Frighten Me*

HOW TO BECOME A WRITER

The Job

Writers are involved with the expression, editing, pro-
moting, and interpreting of ideas and facts. Their work
appears in books, magazines, trade journals, newspapers,
technical studies and reports, company newsletters, radio
and television broadcasts, and even advertisements.

Writers develop ideas for plays, novels, poems, and
other related works. They report, analyze, and interpret
facts, events, and personalities. They also review art,
music, drama, and other artistic presentations. Some writers persuade the general public to choose certain goods,
services, and personalities.

Writers work in the field of communications. Specifi-
cally, they deal with the written word for the printed page,
broadcast, computer screen, or live theater. Their work is
as varied as the materials they produce: books, magazines, trade journals, newspapers, technical reports, com-

pany newsletters and other publications, advertisements, speeches, scripts for motion-picture and stage productions, and for radio and television broadcasts.

Prose writers for newspapers, magazines, and books do many similar tasks. Sometimes they come up with their own idea for an article or book and sometimes they are assigned a topic by an editor. Then they gather as much information as possible about the subject through library research, interviews, the Internet, observation, and other methods. They make notes from which they gather material for their project. Once the material has been organized, they prepare a written outline. The process of developing a piece of writing involves detailed and solitary work, but it is exciting.

When they are working on an assignment, writers submit their outlines to an editor or other company representative for approval. Then they write a first draft of the manuscript, trying to put the material into words that will have the desired effect on their readers. They often rewrite or polish sections of the material, always searching for just the right way of getting the information across or expressing an idea or opinion. A manuscript may be reviewed, corrected, and revised numerous times before a final copy is submitted.

Writers for newspapers, magazines, or books often specialize in a specific subject. Some writers might have an educational background that allows them to give a critical interpretation or analysis. For example, a health or science writer typically has a degree in biology and can interpret new ideas in the field for the average reader.

Screenwriters prepare scripts for motion pictures or television. They select—or are assigned—a subject, conduct research, write and submit a plot outline or story, and discuss possible revisions with the producer and/or director. Screenwriters may adapt books or plays for film and television. They often collaborate with other screenwriters and may specialize in a particular type of script.

Playwrights write for the stage. They create dialogue and describe action for comedies and dramas. Themes are sometimes adapted from fictional, historical, or narrative sources. Playwrights combine action, conflict, purpose, and resolution to tell stories of real or imaginary life. They often make revisions even while the play is in rehearsal.

Continuity writers prepare material for radio and television announcers to introduce or connect various parts of their programs.

Novelists and short-story writers create stories for books, magazines, or literary journals. They use incidents from their own lives, from news events, or from their imagination to create characters, settings, and actions. Poets create narrative, dramatic, or lyric poetry for books, magazines, or other publications, as well as for special events such as commemorations.

Requirements

High School   High-school courses that are helpful for a writer include English, literature, foreign languages, general science, social studies, computer science, and typing. The ability to type and familiarity with computers are almost requisites for positions in communications.

Postsecondary   Competition for work as a writer almost always demands the background of a college education.

Many employers prefer people who have a broad liberal arts background or a major in English, literature, history, philosophy, or one of the social sciences. Some employers prefer communications or journalism training in college. Occasionally a master's degree in a specialized writing field may be required. A number of colleges and schools offer courses in journalism, and some of them offer courses in book publishing, publication management, and newspaper and magazine writing.

In addition to formal education, most employers look for practical writing experience. If you have worked on high-school or college newspapers, yearbooks, or literary magazines, you will make a better candidate. Work for small community newspapers or radio stations, even in an unpaid position, is also an advantage. Many book publishers, magazines, newspapers, and radio and television stations have summer internship programs. These provide valuable training if you want to learn about the publishing and broadcasting businesses. Interns do many simple tasks, such as running errands and answering phones, but some may be asked to perform research, conduct interviews, or even write some minor pieces.

Writers who specialize in technical fields may need degrees, concentrated course work, or experience in their subject areas. This usually applies to engineering, business, and the sciences. Also, a degree in technical communications is now offered at many colleges.

If you want a position with the federal government, you will be required to take a civil service examination and meet specific requirements, according to the type and level of the position.

Other Requirements Writers should be creative and able to express ideas clearly, have broad general knowledge, be skilled in research techniques, and be computer-literate. Other assets include curiosity, persistence, initiative, resourcefulness, and an accurate memory. For some jobs—on a newspaper, for example, where the activity is hectic and the deadlines are short—the ability to concentrate and produce under pressure is essential.

Exploring

As a high-school or college student, you can test your interest and aptitude in the field by working as a reporter or writer on school newspapers, yearbooks, and literary magazines. Various writing courses, workshops, and books help you to sharpen your writing skills.

Small community newspapers and local radio stations often welcome contributions from outside sources, although they may not have the resources to pay for them. Jobs in bookstores, magazine shops, and even newsstands can help you become familiar with the various publications.

Information on writing as a career may also be obtained by visiting local newspapers, publishers, or radio and television stations. You may interview some of the writers who work there. Career conferences and other guidance programs often have speakers on the field of communications from local or national organizations.

Employers

Nearly one-third of salaried writers and editors work for newspapers, magazines, and book publishers, according to the *Occupational Outlook Handbook*. Many writers work for advertising agencies, in radio and television broadcasting, or in public relations firms. Others work on journals and newsletters published by business and non-profit organizations. Other employers include government agencies and film-production companies.

Starting Out

Experience is required to gain a high-level position in this field. Most writers start out in entry-level jobs. These jobs may be listed with college placement offices, or you may apply directly to publishers or broadcasting companies. Graduates who have previously served internships with these companies often know someone who can give them a personal recommendation.

Employers in the communications field are usually interested in samples of your published writing. These may be assembled in an organized portfolio or scrapbook. Bylined or signed articles are more helpful than those whose source is not identified.

A beginning position as a junior writer usually involves library research, preparation of rough drafts for a report, cataloging, and other related writing tasks. These are generally carried on under the supervision of a senior writer.

Advancement

Most writers start out as editorial or production assistants. Advancement is often more rapid in small companies, where beginners learn by doing a little of everything and may be given writing tasks immediately. In large firms, however, duties are usually more compartmentalized. Assistants in entry-level positions do research, fact-checking, and copyrighting, but it generally takes much longer to advance to writing tasks.

Promotion into a more responsible position may come with the assignment of more important articles and stories, or it may be the result of moving to another company. Employees in this field often move around. An assistant in one publishing house may switch to an executive position in another. Or a writer may advance by switching to a related field: for example, from publishing to teaching, public relations, advertising, radio, or television.

Freelance or self-employed writers may advance by earning larger fees as they widen their experience and establish their reputation.

Work Environment

Working conditions vary for writers. Although the workweek usually runs thirty-five to forty hours, many writers work overtime. A publication that is issued frequently has more deadlines closer together, which creates greater pressures. The work is especially hectic on newspapers and at broadcasting companies, which operate seven days a week. Writers often work nights and weekends to meet deadlines or to cover a late-developing story.

Most writers work independently, but often they must cooperate with artists, photographers, rewriters, and advertising people. These people may have widely differing ideas of how the materials should be prepared and presented.

The work is sometimes difficult, but writers are seldom bored. Each day brings new and interesting problems. The jobs occasionally require travel. The most difficult aspect is the pressure of deadlines. People who are the most content as writers enjoy and work well under deadline pressure.

Earnings

In 1998, median annual earning for writers were $36,480 a year, according to the *Occupational Outlook Handbook*. Salaries range from $20,920 to $76,660.

In addition to their salaries, many writers earn some income from freelance work. Part-time freelancers may earn from $5,000 to $15,000 a year. Freelance earnings vary widely. Full-time established freelance writers may earn up to $75,000 a year.

Outlook

Employment in this field is expected to increase faster than the average rate of all occupations through 2008. The demand for writers by newspapers, periodicals, book publishers, and nonprofit organizations is expected to increase.

The major book and magazine publishers, broadcasting companies, advertising agencies, public relations firms, and the federal government account for the large number of writers in cities such as New York, Chicago, Los Angeles, Boston, Philadelphia, San Francisco, and Washington, D.C. Opportunities in small newspapers, corporations, and professional, religious, business, technical, and trade publications can be found throughout the United States.

TO LEARN MORE ABOUT WRITERS

Books

Fletcher, Ralph B. *A Writer's Notebook: Unlocking the Writer within You.* New York: Camelot, 1996.

Janeczko, Paul B. *How to Write Poetry.* New York: Scholastic, 1999.

Krull, Kathleen. *Lives of the Writers: Tragedies, Comedies.* Austin: Raintree/Steck-Vaughn, 1998.

New Moon Books Girls Editorial Board. *Writing: How to Express Yourself with Passion and Practice.* New York: Crown, 2000.

Reeves, Diane Lindsey. *Career Ideas for Kids Who Like Writing.* New York: Facts On File, 1998.

Stevens, Carla. *A Book of Your Own: Keeping a Diary or Journal.* New York: Clarion, 1993.

Websites
Creative Writing for Teens
http://teenwriting.about.com
Tips, news, activities, a chat room, and a selection of young authors' works

4Writers
http://www.4writers.com
Support for professional and aspiring writers, plus information about conferences, artists' colonies, and the top creative writing programs

Writer's Digest
http://www.writersdigest.com
Features daily writing and publishing updates, plus information about the best places to get published

Where to Write
National Association of Science Writers
P.O. Box 294
Greenlawn, NY 11740
516/757-5664
For information on writing and editing careers in the field of communications

National Conference of Editorial Writers
6223 Executive Boulevard
Rockville, MD 20852
301/984-3015
For information about student memberships available to those interested in opinion writing

PEN American Center
568 Broadway
New York, NY 10012-3225
Helps foster writers of literary works and provides awards, grants, and support

Tallwood House
MSN 1E3
George Mason University
Fairfax, VA 22030
Provides support for writers and a directory of writing programs

Writers Guild of America
7000 West Third Street
Los Angeles, CA 90048
For information about this organization that represents writers of all kinds

HOW TO BECOME A FILMMAKER AND DIRECTOR

The Job

The director of a film or television production coordinates all aspects of a film or television show and is responsible for its overall style and quality. Directors are well known for their part in guiding actors, but they are also involved in casting, costuming, cinematography, editing, and sound recording. Directors must have insight into the many special tasks that go into the creation of a film, and they must have a broad vision of how each part will contribute to the big picture.

Motion-picture directors, also called filmmakers, bear the ultimate responsibility for the tone and quality of the films they work on. They interpret the stories and narratives presented in scripts and coordinate the filming. They are involved in preproduction, production, and postproduction. They audition, select, and rehearse the actors; they make decisions regarding set designs, musical scores, and costumes; and they also decide on details such as where scenes should be shot and what backgrounds might be needed. The director of a film often works with a casting director who auditions performers. The casting director studies the attributes of the performers, such as physical appearance, voice quality, and acting ability and experience, and then gives the director a list of suitable candidates.

One of the most important aspects of the film director's job is working with the actors. Directors have their own styles of extracting emotion and performance from cast members, but they must be dedicated to this goal.

The film's art director creates set-design concepts and chooses locations. The art director also is often involved in design ideas for costumes, makeup and hairstyles, photographic effects, and other elements of the film's production.

The director of photography, or cinematographer, organizes and implements the camera work. Together with the filmmaker, he or she interprets scenes and decides on appropriate camera motion. The director of photography determines the lighting required for each shoot and decides on such technical factors as the type of film to be used, camera angles and distance, and focus.

Scenes in motion pictures are not usually filmed in the order of events. As a result, the ending might be shot first and scenes from the middle of the story might not be filmed until the end of production. The director schedules each day's sequence of scenes. The filming is coordinated so that scenes using the same set and performers are filmed together. Filmmakers meet with technicians and crew members to advise on and approve final scenery, lighting, props, and other equipment. They give the final approval of costumes, choreography, and music.

After all the scenes have been shot, postproduction begins. The director then works with picture and sound editors to piece the final reels together. The film editor follows the director's vision of the picture and assembles shots according to that overall idea. The film is synchronized with voice and sound tracks.

The director is assisted by various people throughout the process. The first assistant director organizes practical matters during the shooting of each scene. The second assistant director works as a liaison between the production office, the first assistant director, and the performers. The second unit director coordinates sequences, such as scenic inserts and action shots.

Requirements

High School Film directors' careers do not follow a traditional path. There is no standard training outline involved, and no normal progression up a movie-industry ladder to the director's job. At the very least, a high-school diploma, though not technically required if you wish to become a director, will still probably be indispensable in terms of the background and education it signifies. All artists, especially those in a medium as widely disseminated as film, need to have rich and varied experience in order to create works that are intelligently crafted and speak to people of many different backgrounds. In high school, courses in English, art, theater, and history will give you a good foundation. Further, a high-school diploma will be necessary if you decide to go on to film school. Be active in school and community drama productions.

Postsecondary In college and afterward, take film classes and volunteer to work on other students' films. Dedication, talent, and experience are indispensable to a director. No doubt it is beneficial to become aware of one's passion for film as early as possible. More than 500 film-studies programs are offered by schools of higher education throughout the United States. The most reputable are the American Film Institute in Los Angeles, Columbia University in New York City, New York University (NYU), the University of California at Los Angeles (UCLA), and the University of Southern California (USC). These schools have film professionals on their staff and offer a very visible stage for student talent, being located in the two film-business hot spots—California and New York.

Film school offers overall formal training, providing an education in fundamental directing skills by working with student productions. Such education is rigorous, but in addition to teaching skills it provides aspiring directors with peer groups and a network of contacts with students, faculty, and guest speakers that can be of help after graduation.

Exploring

In high school and beyond, pay attention to motion pictures—watch them at every opportunity, both at the theater and at home. Study your favorite television shows to see what makes them interesting. Major trade publications to read are *Daily Variety* and *Hollywood Reporter*.

Employers

Employment as a film or television director is usually on a freelance or contractual basis. Directors find work with film studios, at television stations and cable networks, through advertising agencies, with record companies, and by creating their own independent film projects.

Starting Out

It is difficult to get started as a motion-picture director. With no traditional steps to professional status, the occupation poses challenges for those seeking employment. However, some solid advice is available for those who wish to direct motion pictures.

Many directors began their careers in other film-industry professions, such as acting or writing. Film school is a great place for making contacts in the industry. Contacts are often the essential factor in getting a job; many Hollywood insiders agree that it's not what you know but who you know that will get you in. Networking often leads to good opportunities at various types of jobs in the industry. Many professionals recommend that those who want to become directors should go to Los Angeles or New York, find any industry-related job, continue to take classes, and keep their eyes and ears open for news of job openings.

One interesting program is the Assistant Directors Training Program of the Directors Guild of America (the address is listed in "To Learn More About Filmmakers and Directors"). This program provides those without industry connections an excellent opportunity to work on film and television productions. Trainees are placed with major studios or on television movies and series. They work for 400 days and earn between $487 and $578 per week, with the salary increasing every 100 days. When they have completed the program, they become freelance second assistant directors and can join the guild. The competition is extremely stiff for admission to this program. Only 16 to 20 trainees are accepted from among some 800 to 1,200 applicants each year.

Advancement

In the motion-picture industry, advancement usually comes with recognition. Directors who work on well-received movies are given awards as well as job offers. Probably the most glamorized trophy is the Academy Award—the Oscar. Oscars are awarded in twenty-four categories, including one for best achievement in directing, and are presented annually.

Work Environment

The director's job is considered glamorous and prestigious, and of course some directors have become famous. But directors work under great stress—meeting deadlines, staying within budgets, and resolving problems among staff. "Nine-to-five" definitely does not describe a day in the life of a director; 16-hour days are common.

Earnings

Directors' salaries vary greatly. Most Hollywood film directors are members of the Directors Guild of America, and salaries (as well as hours of work and other employment conditions) are usually negotiated by this union. Generally, contracts provide for minimum weekly salaries and follow a basic trend depending on the cost of the picture being produced. For example, for film budgets over $1.5 million, the weekly salary is about $8,000; for budgets of $500,000 to $1.5 million, it is $5,800 per week; and for budgets under $500,000, it is $5,100. Motion-picture art directors earn an average weekly salary of about $1,850;

directors of photography get $2,000. Keep in mind that because directors are freelancers, they may have no income for many weeks during the year.

Salaries for directors who work in television vary greatly. They are based on type of project and employer and on whether the director is employed as a freelancer or as a salaried employee. The average annual salary for a director of a television news program is about $50,000. A director at a small-market station may average as little as $28,000 per year, while a director employed by a larger network affiliate may make up to $120,000 annually.

Outlook

According to the U.S. Department of Labor, employment for motion-picture and television directors is expected to grow faster than the average for all occupations through the year 2008. This optimistic forecast is based on the increasing global demand for films and television programming made in the United States, as well as continuing U.S. demand for home-video rentals. However, competition is extreme and turnover is high. Most positions in the motion-picture industry are freelance jobs. Directors are usually hired to work on one film at a time. After a film is completed, new contacts must be made for further assignments.

Television offers directors a wider variety of employment opportunities. For example, they may direct sitcoms, made-for-TV movies, newscasts, commercials—and even music videos. Half of all television directors are freelancers. This number is predicted to rise as more cable networks and production companies try to cut costs by hiring directors on a freelance basis.

TO LEARN MORE ABOUT FILMMAKERS AND DIRECTORS

Books

Ferber, Elizabeth. *Steven Spielberg: A Biography*. Broomall, Penn.: Chelsea House, 1996.

Frantz, John Parris. *Video Cinema: Techniques and Projects for Beginning Filmmakers*. Chicago: Chicago Review Press, 1994.

Hammontree, Marie. *Walt Disney: Young Movie Maker*. New York: Aladdin, 1997.

Hardy, James Earl. *Spike Lee: Filmmaker*. Broomall, Penn.: Chelsea House, 1995.

Hitzeroth, Deborah, and Sharon Heerboth. *Movies: The World on Film*. San Diego: Lucent, 1991.

Rau, Dana Meachen, and Christophe Rau. *George Lucas: Creator of Star Wars*. Danbury, Conn.: Franklin Watts, 1999.

Websites
Association of Independent Video and Filmmakers
http://www.aivf.org/
A vital resource for independent film and video makers

The Directors Guild of America
http://www.dga.org/
The official site of the DGA, a group that serves and protects member rights in the filmmaking industry

UCLA Film and Television Archive
http://www.cinema.ucla.edu/
Contains more than 220,000 films and television programs and newsreel footage; also provides information about admission to UCLA's premiere film school

Where to Write
American Film Institute
P.O. Box 27999
2021 North Western Avenue
Los Angeles, CA 90027
For information about colleges with film and television programs of study

Directors Guild—Assistant Directors Training Program
15503 Ventura Boulevard
Sherman Oaks, CA 91436-2140
For information about the Assistant Directors Training Program

TO LEARN MORE ABOUT MAYA ANGELOU

Books

King, Sarah E. *Maya Angelou: Greeting the Morning.* Brookfield, Conn.: Millbrook Press, 1994.

Kite, L. Patricia. *Maya Angelou.* New York: Lerner, 1999.

Loos, Pamela. *Maya Angelou.* Broomall, Penn.: Chelsea House, 1999.

Pettit, Jane. *Maya Angelou: Journey of the Heart.* New York: Puffin Books, 1996.

Shapiro, Miles. *Maya Angelou.* Broomall, Penn.: Chelsea House, 1994.

Spain, Valerie. *Meet Maya Angelou.* New York: Random House, 1994.

Websites

Maya Angelou—Greatness through Literature
http://www.wic.org/bio/mangelou.htm
A brief biography provided as part of the Women's International Center site

Timeline of the American Civil Rights Movement
http://www.wmich.edu/politics/mlk/
A site created to honor Martin Luther King Jr. Provides an overview of the civil rights movement in the United States

Voices from the Gap—Maya Angelou
http://voices.cla.umn.edu/authors/MayaAngelou.html
A biography and bibliography provided by Voices from the Gap, a group that focuses on writing by women of color

Interesting Places to Visit
The Museum of Television and Radio
25 West 52nd Street
New York, NY 10019
212/621-6600

National Public Broadcasting Archives
University of Maryland
College Park, MD 20742
301/405-0800

Schomberg Center for Research in Black Culture
515 Malcolm X Boulevard
New York, NY 10037-1801
212/491-2200

Z. Smith Reynolds Library
Maya Angelou Papers
Wake Forest University
Winston-Salem, NC 27109
336/758-5201 (for a campus tour)
336/758-5755 (for information about Angelou's papers)

INDEX

Page numbers in *italics* indicate illustrations.

ABOUT THE AUTHOR

Lucia Raatma received her bachelor's degree in English literature from the University of South Carolina and her master's degree in cinema studies from New York University. Both degrees taught her the power of stories, and very often she feels that the best stories are true ones. She found Maya Angelou's life to be one of strength and courage, a tribute to the power of the human spirit.

Lucia Raatma has written a wide range of books for young people. They include *Libraries* and *How Books Are Made* (Children's Press); an eight-book general-safety series and a four-book fire-safety series (Bridgestone Books); and fourteen titles in a character-education series (Bridgestone Books). She has also written career biographies of Charles Lindbergh and Bill Gates for this series.

When she is not researching or writing, she enjoys going to movies, playing tennis, and spending time with her husband, daughter, and golden retriever.